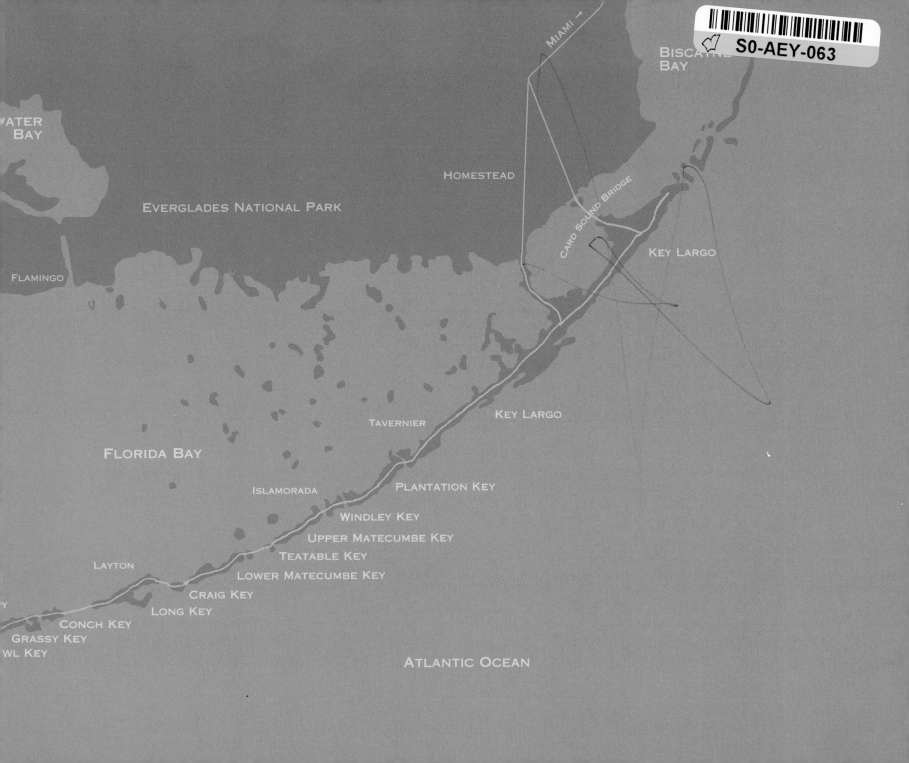

The Florida Keys

KEY LARGO TO KEY WEST

Cheri Howard

Craig & Cheri Howard

Front Cover: Sunrise at Islamorada
Back Cover: View from Fort Jefferson, Dry Tortugas National Park

Copyright ©2003 Craig and Cheri Howard
Two underwater images ©Tom & Therisa Stack

Designed and Published: Craig Howard at Fonts & Film
1103 Truman Avenue, Key West, FL
email: craighowardkeywest@yahoo.com

Printed in Hong Kong

ISBN: 0-9713531-1-5

Niles Channel from Ramrod Key

Sombrero Beach, Marathon ~ Key Vaca

Dolphin Research Center ~ Grassy Key

Trap Boat, Card Sound Road ~ Key Largo

Lobster Boat, Niles Channel ~ Summerland Key

Land Crab ~ Big Torch Key

Magnificent Frigate Birds ~ Dry Tortugas National Park

Snowy Egrets, Wild Bird Center ~ Tavernier

Juvenile Ibis, Wild Bird Center ~ Tavernier

Osprey ~ Big Coppitt Key

Bat Tower and Airport ~ Lower Sugarloaf Key

Fishing Camp on Whale Harbor Channel ~ Windley Key

Flats Fishing ~ Near Teatable Key

Kids Karnival ~ West Summerland Key

4th of July ~ Key West

Curry Hammock State Park ~ Little Crawl Key

Community Park ~ Key Colony Beach

Mallory Square at Port of Key West

Raccoon ~ Middle Torch Key

Juvenile Key Deer ~ Big Pine Key

Beaches at Bahia Honda State Park ~ Bahia Honda Key

San Pedro Catholic Church, Islamorada ~ Plantation Key

Pioneer Cemetery, Islamorada ~ Upper Matecumbe Key

Florida Keys National Marine Sanctuary

Historic Railroad Camp at Pigeon Key

Sandhill Crane ~ Big Pine Key

Red-Bellied Woodpecker ~ No Name Key

Shrimp Boat Dock ~ Stock Island

Old and New Channel Two Bridge ~ Craig Key

Old Long Key Bridge ~ Conch Key

Card Sound Bridge ~ Key Largo

Old and New Seven Mile Bridge, Marathon ~ Knight Key

Oceanside View at Dusk ~ Windley Key

View from Indian Key Channel ~ Near Craig Key

Iguana and Oleander Moth ~ Big Pine Key

Key West Seaport ~ Key West

Ibis in Flight ~ Bahia Honda State Park

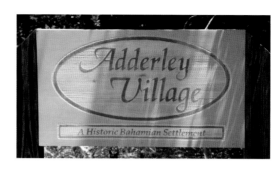

Young Skippers at Helm of the Western Union ~ Key West

Charter Fishing Boats at Holiday Isle Marina ~ Windley Key

Seven Mile Bridge Run ~ Marathon to Little Duck Key

Christ of the Abyss Statue

John Pennekamp Coral Reef State Park ~ Key Largo

APBA Power Boat Races ~ Key West

Kite Surfing ~ Key Largo

Boardwalk and Spider Lily at Long Key State Park ~ Long Key

Zebra Longwing (Florida's State Butterfly) ~ Cudjoe Key

Silver Argiope Spider, Crane Point Hammock ~ Marathon

Fort Jefferson ~ Dry Tortugas National Park

Sea Lion and Dolphins at Theater of the Sea, Islamorada ~ Windley Key

Picnic Island ~ Near Little Torch Key

Sundog (Parhelion Effect) in Morning Sky ~ Saddle Bunch Keys

GULF OF MEXICO

CAPE

FORT JEFFERSON AND
THE DRY TORTUGAS NATIONAL PARK
70 MILES DUE WEST OF KEY WEST

U.S. HIGHWAY 1
KEY WEST TO MIAMI 160 MILES

TORCH
KEYS

SUGARLOAF
KEYS

KE
BE

MARATHON

NO NAME
KEY

BIG COPPITT
KEY

CUDJOE
KEY

SEVEN MILE BRIDGE

KEY
WEST

RAMROD
KEY

BIG PINE
KEY

BAHIA
HONDA

PIGEON KEY

KEY VACA

SADDLEBUNCH KEYS

STOCK
ISLAND

BOCA CHICA
KEY

SUMMERLAND
KEY

WEST
SUMMERLAND KEY